T0275240

This
Planner
Belongs
to

_____

INTRODUCTION

Growing up in England, I remember often being lost while my dad drove around. It was decades before GPS would be available, and oh how I felt its absence! Round and round we would go. Sometimes literally round and round at a roundabout, not sure which turn to take. I'd love to say we all laughed about it, but I remember the tension was palpable. One particular evening, we became so turned around that after hours of searching, we gave up and drove back home—never finding our destination.

On those myriad occasions I remember my dad would say, "I feel that it's down here!" And he meant it. So, off we'd go down some dodgy road. Eventually I felt like Inigo Montoya in *The Princess Bride*, thinking to myself, "I do not think those words mean what you think they mean!"

Perhaps in part because of these formative experiences, I came to one of the most important insights of my life:

There are two kinds of people in the world:
people who are lost
and people who know they are lost.

I seek to be in the second category. I don't claim to be the embodiment of an Essentialist. What I can claim is this: I am willing to admit, every morning, that I feel lost again. And admitting that helps me get back into the arena and tackle the many demands and responsibilities of my life just as we all do.

I am with you on this journey.

Here's the thing: if you're lost and you know you're lost, you are not lost anymore. Even if you have to stop and ask directions a few times, you will eventually find your way to where you want to be.

On the other hand, if you're lost but you don't admit it, then you stay lost. If you say, "I feel it's down here," instead of stopping for directions, you will stay lost.

It wasn't until years later that I learned that even planes are off track 90 percent of the time. They only get to where they are going because they keep getting back on track. That is the purpose of *The Essentialism Planner*: to help bring us back to what's essential day after day. This planner acknowledges that life, much like flying, is full of unexpected deviations. By committing to using this planner every day for 90 days, you are embarking on a voyage of continuous realignment to what's essential.

As you delve into the pages of *The Essentialism Planner*, you are not merely planning your days; you are curating your life. Each page is an invitation to pause, reflect, and choose intentionally. It encourages you to ask yourself whether what you are about to commit to is absolutely essential. This daily practice of discernment and focus is what propels you toward achieving more by doing less. It is a journey of shedding the nonessential to make room for what truly ignites your passion and purpose.

In embracing *The Essentialism Planner*, you join a community of thinkers, doers, and dreamers who have dared to defy the conventional wisdom of "more is better." You become part of a movement that champions the elegance of simplicity, the strength of focus, and the joy of discovering that in the essence of less lies the abundance of a life well-lived. Let this planner be your guide, your compass, and your constant companion as you navigate the beautiful complexity of life, always coming back to what is essential, day after day.

The basic value proposition of Essentialism: only once you give yourself permission to stop trying to do it all, to stop saying yes to everyone, can you make your highest contribution toward the things that really matter.

—*Essentialism*, p. 4

THE WAY OF THE ESSENTIALIST

How often do you say yes simply to please? Or to avoid trouble? Or because "yes" has just become your default response?

Do you ever feel busy but not productive? Like you're always in motion but never getting anywhere?

If you answered yes to any of these, the way out is *The Essentialism Planner*.

This planner will help you with **the relentless pursuit of less but better** in a disciplined way.

The way of the Essentialist is about pausing constantly to ask, **"Am I investing in the right activities?"** The fact is that most activities and opportunities are trivial, and few are vital. The way of the Essentialist involves learning to tell the difference—learning to filter through all those options and selecting only those that are truly essential. It's not about how to get more things done; it's about how to get the right things done. You want to make the wisest possible investment of your time and energy so that you can operate at your highest point of contribution by doing only what is essential.

THE ESSENTIALIST'S PLANNER

Becoming an Essentialist is an active daily process. Just like the pursuit of any lifestyle, it takes retraining your brain to let go of old habits that reinforce nonessential goals and tasks and to instead adopt Essentialist thinking. This planner introduces you to the philosophy of Essentialism and helps you put it to practice for 90 days. Rather than filling your planner with meaningless tasks and activities, you'll be challenged every day for 90 days to let go of the nonessential so you can focus on what's most essential. Focus your planner on what's essential this quarter—and use every day's planning grid to inch closer to it while you eliminate distractions. Before long, you'll find it becomes second nature to give yourself permission to stop trying to do it all and to stop saying yes to everyone. And at the end of the 90 days, you'll hopefully achieve what you set out to do or you'll have the clarity on what comes next.

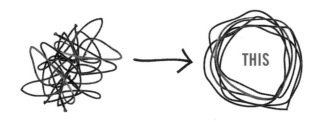

	NONESSENTIALIST	ESSENTIALIST
See	**EVERYTHING TO EVERYONE** "I have to" "It's all important" "If I can fit it in, I should fit it in"	**LESS BUT BETTER** "I choose to" "Only a few things really matter" "What are the trade-offs?"
Do	**THE UNDISCIPLINED PURSUIT OF MORE** Reacts to what's most pressing Says yes to people without really thinking Tries to force execution at the last moment	**THE DISCIPLINED PURSUIT OF LESS** Pauses to discern what really matters Says no to everything except the essential Removes obstacles to make execution easier
Get	**PLATEAU IN YOUR PROGRESS** Feels out of control Unsure of whether the right things got done Experiences overwhelm and exhaustion	**DO SOMETHING TRULY GREAT** Feels in control Gets the right things done Enjoys the journey

The
Personal
Quarterly
Offsite

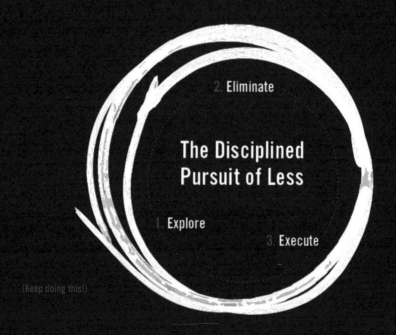

2. Eliminate

The Disciplined
Pursuit of Less

1. Explore

3. Execute

(Keep doing this!)

Holding a Personal Quarterly Offsite is a way to see what's happening in our lives, why it matters, and what we need to focus on next.

It's a chance to get away from the reactive, meeting-to-meeting pulse that can lead to otherwise intelligent people being tricked by the trivial.

Every 90 days you take a day to go somewhere away from the deafening digital noise and usual routine of your busy life and reflect on what really matters.

If you can't take a day, try devoting a few hours on the weekend to think about three big questions:

1. What's essential that I'm underinvesting in?
2. What's nonessential that I'm overinvesting in?
3. How can I make it effortless to get the most important things done?

When we don't take time to ask these more strategic questions, we become a function of other people's agendas. We are left to react to the latest email and can become rudderless, blown about by every wind of change.

The following pages will take you through this quarter's personal offsite. By the time you get to the end of this section, you will have clarity on what important adjustments you want to make over the next 90 days.

EXPLORE: WHAT IS ESSENTIAL?

> What is something essential you are underinvesting in?

▶ Why is this important to you?
Why?
Why?
Why?
Why?

What does success look like for you over the next 90 days?

How many minutes/hours per week would it take to make this happen?

ELIMINATE: WHAT IS NONESSENTIAL?

> What are some nonessential activities you are overinvesting in?

▶ Why are you spending time on these activities?
Why?
Why?
Why?
Why?

▶ How much time did you spend on them over the last 90 days?

What is the full price (financial, emotional, mental) you are paying for them?

EXECUTE: HOW CAN THIS BE EASY?

▶ Who do you need to talk with to make this happen?

▶ What really matters to them right now?

▶ What would make this a win-win?

▶ How can you say what you want in terms of their agenda?

The Essentialist's Daily Planner

WHAT? What is going on in my life?

_____

_____

_____

_____

_____

_____

_____

SO WHAT? Why does all this matter?

_____

_____

_____

_____

If you don't prioritize your life, someone else will.

—*Essentialism*, p. 10

NOW WHAT? What's important now?

1 essential project

- _____

2 urgent and essential tasks

- _____
- _____

3 maintenance items

- _____
- _____
- _____

Other tasks or notes

- _____
- _____
- _____
- _____
- _____
- _____
- _____
- _____

THE POWER HALF AN HOUR

Have you ever felt bombarded by the amount of noise there is in the world today? I don't mean literal noise, but all the digital noise, the internal mental noise, and the noise between people that makes it hard to even understand what somebody else is thinking. In a world of constant commotion and distraction, it is essential that we learn how to eliminate the noise so we can better hear the signal that is leading us toward our highest potential.

Enter the Power Half an Hour*, which kick-starts every daily page in this planner. During this dedicated time of 30 minutes, you will synthesize thoughts, gain clarity, and uncover deeper insights into complex issues. This time allows you to focus on what truly matters and can be particularly effective when facing challenging decisions or when seeking to understand the core of a situation.

One simple structure will help you plan, ponder, and synthesize what's going on in your life.

WHAT? What is going on in my life?

List all your important projects, tasks, and responsibilities. If you are having trouble getting started, reflect on a single question that you want to explore—a professional challenge, a personal decision, or a philosophical inquiry.

SO WHAT? Why does all this matter?

This is a connect-the-dots question: What does all of this mean? Imagine you're a journalist writing a headline for your life. What is the news in your life? What is the headline? Once I wrote, "You're overwhelmed: it's time to breathe" in answer to this question. Another time I wrote, "Work" as my headline because I felt clear about what was essential but now it was time to make it happen.

NOW WHAT? What's important now?

Once you know what's important and why, it's time to design your day. The 1-2-3 Method®
(see opposite page) will help you do this as effortlessly as possible.

---

* During your Power Half an Hour, disconnect from email notifications, texting, and news updates. Disconnecting from technology prevents you from diving headlong into the noise of the day and allows for deeper introspection.

THE 1-2-3 METHOD®

Do you ever feel like life is living you instead of you living it?

Often, life seems like a giant game of reaction, requiring you to jump from one task to another while still trying to achieve what's important. And somehow, we believe if we can just optimize our schedule, cut out downtime, and multitask—we can get it all done. But the truth is it's a juggling act none of us can keep up with.

The answer, paradoxically, doesn't lie in figuring out how to do more things in less time. It lies in figuring out how to do fewer things better. When you can clearly see and prioritize the many things in your life, you can begin to build a rhythm that gives you control and order, allowing you to live a life you design.

The 1-2-3 Method® helps you answer the question ***Now What?*** It is a daily method you can use to take back control of your day and make this complex dance between the urgent and the essential easier to navigate. It's simple on the surface but profound in its impact. In this planner, you'll use this method daily.

Here's how it works. Identify:

ONE essential project and work on it for three hours. This is today's priority.

TWO urgent and essential tasks that must get done to keep you from falling behind.

THREE maintenance items to complete to stay organized and prevent problems.

The rhythm of our lives and the weight of our choices hinge on a simple understanding—clarity in prioritization. Yet, as the demands of our modern age increase, we often find ourselves juggling the urgent with the essential. This dance, while complex, becomes easier to navigate with the 1-2-3 Method®.

For more info on the Power Half an Hour, check out episode 233 of my podcast. To learn more about the 1-2-3 Method®, listen to episode 225.

WHAT? What is going on in my life?

_____

_____

_____

_____

_____

_____

_____

SO WHAT? Why does all this matter?

_____

_____

_____

_____

If you don't prioritize your life, someone else will.

—*Essentialism*, p. 10

NOW WHAT? What's important now?

1 essential project

- _____

2 urgent and essential tasks

- _____

- _____

3 maintenance items

- _____

- _____

- _____

Other tasks or notes

- _____

- _____

- _____

- _____

- _____

- _____

- _____

- _____

TUESDAY ___ / ___

WHAT? What is going on in my life?

_____

_____

_____

_____

_____

_____

_____

SO WHAT? Why does all this matter?

_____

_____

_____

_____

TODAY'S CHALLENGE:

Nonessentialists forfeit the right to choose. Essentialists exercise the power of choice. Today, catch yourself saying the words, "I have to." Replace them with, "I choose to."

—*Essentialism,* p. 39

NOW WHAT? What's important now?

1 essential project

- _____

2 urgent and essential tasks

- _____
- _____

3 maintenance items

- _____
- _____
- _____

Other tasks or notes

- _____
- _____
- _____
- _____
- _____
- _____
- _____
- _____

WHAT? What is going on in my life?

_____

_____

_____

_____

_____

_____

_____

SO WHAT? Why does all this matter?

_____

_____

_____

_____

> **Perfectionism makes essential projects hard to start, self-doubt makes them hard to finish, and trying to do too much, too fast, makes it hard to sustain momentum.**
>
> —*Effortless*, p. 16

NOW WHAT? What's important now?

1 essential project

- _____

2 urgent and essential tasks

- _____

- _____

3 maintenance items

- _____

- _____

- _____

Other tasks or notes

- _____

- _____

- _____

- _____

- _____

- _____

- _____

- _____

WHAT? What is going on in my life?

_____

_____

_____

_____

_____

_____

_____

SO WHAT? Why does all this matter?

_____

_____

_____

_____

TODAY'S CHALLENGE:

What is one small change you can commit to over the next seven days?
What difference do you hope it will make? Why is that important to you?

—_1-Minute Wednesday Newsletter_

NOW WHAT? What's important now?

1 essential project

- _____

2 urgent and essential tasks

- _____

- _____

3 maintenance items

- _____

- _____

- _____

Other tasks or notes

- _____

- _____

- _____

- _____

- _____

- _____

- _____

- _____

WHAT? What is going on in my life?

_____

_____

_____

_____

_____

_____

_____

SO WHAT? Why does all this matter?

_____

_____

_____

_____

Start in the smallest possible way: Block some time, block some blank space, go on a walk, get away—and make it repetitive so that you can create space to really think.

—*1-Minute Wednesday Newsletter*

NOW WHAT? What's important now?

1 essential project

- _____

2 urgent and essential tasks

- _____

- _____

3 maintenance items

- _____

- _____

- _____

Other tasks or notes

- _____

- _____

- _____

- _____

- _____

- _____

- _____

- _____

WHAT? What is going on in my life?

_____

_____

_____

_____

_____

_____

_____

SO WHAT? Why does all this matter?

_____

_____

_____

_____

TODAY'S CHALLENGE:

Take a moment to notice:
- How often are you prioritizing connection with people miles away over the essential relationships with those around you?

You don't need to make a big shift in your behavior today. Just observe.

—*1-Minute Wednesday Newsletter*

NOW WHAT? What's important now?

1 essential project

- _____

2 urgent and essential tasks

- _____

- _____

3 maintenance items

- _____

- _____

- _____

Other tasks or notes

- _____

- _____

- _____

- _____

- _____

- _____

- _____

- _____

WHAT? What is going on in my life?

_____

_____

_____

_____

_____

_____

SO WHAT? Why does all this matter?

_____

_____

_____

_____

What if we stopped celebrating being busy as a measurement of importance? What if instead we celebrated how much time we had spent listening, pondering, meditating, and enjoying time with the most important people in our lives?

—*Essentialism*, p. 26

NOW WHAT? What's important now?

1 essential project

- _____

2 urgent and essential tasks

- _____

- _____

3 maintenance items

- _____

- _____

- _____

Other tasks or notes

- _____

- _____

- _____

- _____

- _____

- _____

- _____

- _____

Weekly
REFLECTION

STEP 1.
PRACTICE RADICAL GRATITUDE

Review the last week and write down five things you're
grateful for (including the tough things).

- _____

- _____

- _____

- _____

- _____

STEP 2.
PREVIEW THE WEEK

Review your calendar and write down the major events
or activities already scheduled for the coming week.

- _____

- _____

- _____

- _____

- _____

INVEST INTENTIONALLY AND DIVEST DELIBERATELY

Write down two to three essentials you're currently underinvesting in.

- _____
- _____
- _____

Write down two to three nonessentials you're currently overinvesting in.

- _____
- _____
- _____

NOW, CHOOSE THIS WEEK'S GOALS

Capture the three essential items you want to accomplish over the coming week.

- _____
- _____
- _____

WHAT? What is going on in my life?

_____

_____

_____

_____

_____

_____

_____

SO WHAT? Why does all this matter?

_____

_____

_____

_____

> **We overvalue nonessentials like a nicer car or house, or even intangibles like the number of our followers on Twitter or the way we look in our Facebook photos. As a result, we neglect activities that _are_ truly essential, like spending time with our loved ones, or nurturing our spirit, or taking care of our health.**
>
> —_Essentialism_, p. 123

NOW WHAT? What's important now?

1 essential project

- _____

2 urgent and essential tasks

- _____

- _____

3 maintenance items

- _____

- _____

- _____

Other tasks or notes

- _____

- _____

- _____

- _____

- _____

- _____

- _____

- _____

WHAT? What is going on in my life?

_____

_____

_____

_____

_____

_____

_____

SO WHAT? Why does all this matter?

_____

_____

_____

_____

TODAY'S CHALLENGE:

Making the essential automatic is crucial for living an essential life. But automation can work against us (i.e., a subscription service you pay for but no longer use). Identify one form of negative automation in your life and eliminate it.

—_1-Minute Wednesday Newsletter_

NOW WHAT? What's important now?

1 essential project

- _____

2 urgent and essential tasks

- _____

- _____

3 maintenance items

- _____

- _____

- _____

Other tasks or notes

- _____

- _____

- _____

- _____

- _____

- _____

- _____

- _____

WHAT? What is going on in my life?

_____

_____

_____

_____

_____

_____

_____

SO WHAT? Why does all this matter?

_____

_____

_____

_____

The way of the Essentialist is the path to being in control of our own choices. It is a path to new levels of success and meaning. It is the path on which we enjoy the journey, not just the destination.

—*Essentialism*, p. 9

NOW WHAT? What's important now?

1 essential project

- _____

2 urgent and essential tasks

- _____

- _____

3 maintenance items

- _____

- _____

- _____

Other tasks or notes

- _____

- _____

- _____

- _____

- _____

- _____

- _____

- _____

WHAT? What is going on in my life?

_____

_____

_____

_____

_____

_____

_____

SO WHAT? Why does all this matter?

_____

_____

_____

_____

TODAY'S CHALLENGE:

Taking time to reflect on what matters to you each day will change your day. And when you do this consistently, it will change your life:

- Block out 10 minutes at the beginning of your day and make a list of what matters to you today.
- Prioritize the list and reference it throughout the day.
- Reflect on how you did.

—1-Minute Wednesday Newsletter

NOW WHAT? What's important now?

1 essential project

- _____

2 urgent and essential tasks

- _____

- _____

3 maintenance items

- _____

- _____

- _____

Other tasks or notes

- _____

- _____

- _____

- _____

- _____

- _____

- _____

- _____

WHAT? What is going on in my life?

_____

_____

_____

_____

_____

_____

_____

SO WHAT? Why does all this matter?

_____

_____

_____

_____

The way of the Essentialist is the relentless pursuit of less but better. It doesn't mean occasionally giving a nod to the principle. It means pursuing it in a _disciplined_ way.

—*Essentialism*, p. 5

NOW WHAT? What's important now?

1 essential project

- _____

2 urgent and essential tasks

- _____

- _____

3 maintenance items

- _____

- _____

- _____

Other tasks or notes

- _____

- _____

- _____

- _____

- _____

- _____

- _____

- _____

WHAT? What is going on in my life?

_____

_____

_____

_____

_____

_____

_____

SO WHAT? Why does all this matter?

_____

_____

_____

_____

TODAY'S CHALLENGE:

Though it has never been easier to connect or reconnect with family members and old friends, many of us feel more isolated than ever. The solution to feeling more connected is not more social interactions; it's more meaningful interactions. Think of someone important in your life and reach out to them today. It will make both of your lives better.

—_1-Minute Wednesday Newsletter_

NOW WHAT? What's important now?

1 essential project

- _____

2 urgent and essential tasks

- _____

- _____

3 maintenance items

- _____

- _____

- _____

Other tasks or notes

- _____

- _____

- _____

- _____

- _____

- _____

- _____

- _____

WHAT? What is going on in my life?

_____

_____

_____

_____

_____

_____

SO WHAT? Why does all this matter?

_____

_____

_____

_____

> Play might seem like a nonessential activity. Often it is treated that way. But in fact play *is* essential in many ways. Stuart Brown, the founder of the National Institute for Play, has studied what are called the play histories of some six thousand individuals and has concluded that play has the power to significantly improve everything from personal health to relationships to education to organizations' ability to innovate.
>
> —*Essentialism*, p. 85

NOW WHAT? What's important now?

1 essential project

- _____

2 urgent and essential tasks

- _____

- _____

3 maintenance items

- _____

- _____

- _____

Other tasks or notes

- _____

- _____

- _____

- _____

- _____

- _____

- _____

- _____

Weekly
REFLECTION

STEP 1.
PRACTICE RADICAL GRATITUDE

Review the last week and write down five things you're
grateful for (including the tough things).

- _____

- _____

- _____

- _____

- _____

STEP 2.
PREVIEW THE WEEK

Review your calendar and write down the major events
or activities already scheduled for the coming week.

- _____

- _____

- _____

- _____

- _____

INVEST INTENTIONALLY AND DIVEST DELIBERATELY

Write down two to three essentials you're currently underinvesting in.

- _____

- _____

- _____

Write down two to three nonessentials you're currently overinvesting in.

- _____

- _____

- _____

STEP 4.

NOW, CHOOSE THIS WEEK'S GOALS

Capture the three essential items you want to accomplish over the coming week.

- _____

- _____

- _____

WHAT? What is going on in my life?

_____

_____

_____

_____

_____

_____

_____

SO WHAT? Why does all this matter?

_____

_____

_____

_____

If it isn't a clear *yes,* then it's a clear *no.*

—*Essentialism,* p. 109

NOW WHAT? What's important now?

1 essential project

- _____

2 urgent and essential tasks

- _____

- _____

3 maintenance items

- _____

- _____

- _____

Other tasks or notes

- _____

- _____

- _____

- _____

- _____

- _____

- _____

- _____

WHAT? What is going on in my life?

_____

_____

_____

_____

_____

_____

SO WHAT? Why does all this matter?

_____

_____

_____

_____

TODAY'S CHALLENGE:

There is a space between agreeing and disagreeing, and in that space lies our ability to understand each other. Today, resist the urge to make your position known in every conversation. Ask yourself instead, How often do I approach a conversation with the intent of agreeing or disagreeing?

—*The Greg McKeown Podcast,* episode 231, "The Disciplined Pursuit of Doing Nothing"

NOW WHAT? What's important now?

1 essential project

- _____

2 urgent and essential tasks

- _____

- _____

3 maintenance items

- _____

- _____

- _____

Other tasks or notes

- _____

- _____

- _____

- _____

- _____

- _____

- _____

- _____

WHAT? What is going on in my life?

_____

_____

_____

_____

_____

_____

_____

SO WHAT? Why does all this matter?

_____

_____

_____

_____

> **Research has shown that of all forms of human motivation the most effective one is progress. Why? Because a small, concrete win creates momentum and affirms our faith in our further success.**
>
> —*Essentialism,* p. 196

NOW WHAT? What's important now?

1 essential project

- _____

2 urgent and essential tasks

- _____

- _____

3 maintenance items

- _____

- _____

- _____

Other tasks or notes

- _____

- _____

- _____

- _____

- _____

- _____

- _____

- _____

THURSDAY ___ / ___

WHAT? What is going on in my life?

_____

_____

_____

_____

_____

_____

_____

SO WHAT? Why does all this matter?

_____

_____

_____

_____

TODAY'S CHALLENGE:

When things become automatic, they become easier (like automating bill pay). Make your life easier through automation.

- Think about a decision you make often.
- Determine how you want to handle it moving forward.
- Identify how to automate it.

—1-Minute Wednesday Newsletter

NOW WHAT? What's important now?

1 essential project

- _____

2 urgent and essential tasks

- _____

- _____

3 maintenance items

- _____

- _____

- _____

Other tasks or notes

- _____

- _____

- _____

- _____

- _____

- _____

- _____

- _____

WHAT? What is going on in my life?

_____

_____

_____

_____

_____

_____

_____

SO WHAT? Why does all this matter?

_____

_____

_____

_____

> **There should be no shame in admitting to a mistake; after all, we really are only admitting that we are now wiser than we once were.**
>
> —*Essentialism,* p. 150

NOW WHAT? What's important now?

1 essential project

- _____

2 urgent and essential tasks

- _____

- _____

3 maintenance items

- _____

- _____

- _____

Other tasks or notes

- _____

- _____

- _____

- _____

- _____

- _____

- _____

- _____

WHAT? What is going on in my life?

_____

_____

_____

_____

_____

_____

_____

SO WHAT? Why does all this matter?

_____

_____

_____

_____

TODAY'S CHALLENGE:

What if doing less was actually more effective than giving 100%? Make a list of projects or areas where you often feel like you need to give 110%. Now list what 85% effort would look like in these areas. What mindset shifts do you need to make to embrace the 85% Rule?

—*The Greg McKeown Podcast,* episode 258, "The 85% Rule"

NOW WHAT? What's important now?

1 essential project

- _____

2 urgent and essential tasks

- _____

- _____

3 maintenance items

- _____

- _____

- _____

Other tasks or notes

- _____

- _____

- _____

- _____

- _____

- _____

- _____

- _____

WHAT? What is going on in my life?

_____

_____

_____

_____

_____

_____

_____

SO WHAT? Why does all this matter?

_____

_____

_____

_____

> **Reading a book is among the most high-leverage activities on earth. For an investment more or less equivalent to the length of a single workday (and a few dollars), you can gain access to what the smartest people have already figured out.**
>
> —*Effortless*, p. 162

NOW WHAT? What's important now?

1 essential project

- _____

2 urgent and essential tasks

- _____

- _____

3 maintenance items

- _____

- _____

- _____

Other tasks or notes

- _____

- _____

- _____

- _____

- _____

- _____

- _____

- _____

Weekly
REFLECTION

STEP 1.
PRACTICE RADICAL GRATITUDE

Review the last week and write down five things you're
grateful for (including the tough things).

- _____

- _____

- _____

- _____

- _____

STEP 2.
PREVIEW THE WEEK

Review your calendar and write down the major events
or activities already scheduled for the coming week.

- _____

- _____

- _____

- _____

- _____

INVEST INTENTIONALLY AND DIVEST DELIBERATELY

Write down two to three essentials you're currently underinvesting in.

- _____
- _____
- _____

Write down two to three nonessentials you're currently overinvesting in.

- _____
- _____
- _____

NOW, CHOOSE THIS WEEK'S GOALS

Capture the three essential items you want to accomplish over the coming week.

- _____
- _____
- _____

WHAT? What is going on in my life?

_____

_____

_____

_____

_____

_____

_____

SO WHAT? Why does all this matter?

_____

_____

_____

_____

**A Nonessentialist thinks almost everything is essential.
An Essentialist thinks almost everything is nonessential.**

—*Essentialism*, p. 46–47

NOW WHAT? What's important now?

1 essential project

- _____

2 urgent and essential tasks

- _____

- _____

3 maintenance items

- _____

- _____

- _____

Other tasks or notes

- _____

- _____

- _____

- _____

- _____

- _____

- _____

- _____

WHAT? What is going on in my life?

_____

_____

_____

_____

_____

_____

_____

SO WHAT? Why does all this matter?

_____

_____

_____

_____

TODAY'S CHALLENGE:

What distinguishes top performers in any organization is not their busyness but their ability to focus on what matters and do that consistently over time. Here's how to start doing this:

1. **Become clear on what's essential:** List your top priority in your professional and personal life.
2. **Become clear on why it is important:** Why does this matter so much?
3. **Communicate:** Tell others, "This is the priority project that I am working on. And this is the reason it matters so much."

—*1-Minute Wednesday Newsletter*

NOW WHAT? What's important now?

1 essential project

- _____

2 urgent and essential tasks

- _____

- _____

3 maintenance items

- _____

- _____

- _____

Other tasks or notes

- _____

- _____

- _____

- _____

- _____

- _____

- _____

- _____

WHAT? What is going on in my life?

_____

_____

_____

_____

_____

_____

_____

SO WHAT? Why does all this matter?

_____

_____

_____

_____

> **We can either make our choices deliberately or allow other people's agendas to control our lives.**
>
> —*Essentialism*, p. 16

NOW WHAT? What's important now?

1 essential project

- _____

2 urgent and essential tasks

- _____

- _____

3 maintenance items

- _____

- _____

- _____

Other tasks or notes

- _____

- _____

- _____

- _____

- _____

- _____

- _____

- _____

WHAT? What is going on in my life?

_____

_____

_____

_____

_____

_____

_____

SO WHAT? Why does all this matter?

_____

_____

_____

_____

TODAY'S CHALLENGE:

Holding back when we have "more in the tank" is vital in achieving breakthrough results. . . . Find consistent, steady progress by setting an upper and lower bound with this rule: **Never less than X, never more than Y.** Finding the right range allows you to develop a rhythm. Progress begins to flow, and your actions begin to feel effortless.

—_1-Minute Wednesday Newsletter_

NOW WHAT? What's important now?

1 essential project

- _____

2 urgent and essential tasks

- _____

- _____

3 maintenance items

- _____

- _____

- _____

Other tasks or notes

- _____

- _____

- _____

- _____

- _____

- _____

- _____

- _____

WHAT? What is going on in my life?

_____

_____

_____

_____

_____

_____

_____

SO WHAT? Why does all this matter?

_____

_____

_____

_____

> Essentialism is about how to get the _right_ things done. It is about making the wisest possible investment of your time and energy in order to operate at our highest point of contribution by doing only what is essential.

—*Essentialism,* p. 5

NOW WHAT? What's important now?

1 essential project

- _____

2 urgent and essential tasks

- _____

- _____

3 maintenance items

- _____

- _____

- _____

Other tasks or notes

- _____

- _____

- _____

- _____

- _____

- _____

- _____

- _____

WHAT? What is going on in my life?

_____

_____

_____

_____

_____

_____

_____

SO WHAT? Why does all this matter?

_____

_____

_____

_____

TODAY'S CHALLENGE:

Most of us approach simplification in the wrong way. We start with something complex and try to make it simpler. Instead, try taking the opposite approach today: **Start with zero and then add back only the necessary steps.**

—*1-Minute Wednesday Newsletter*

NOW WHAT? What's important now?

1 essential project

- _____

2 urgent and essential tasks

- _____

- _____

3 maintenance items

- _____

- _____

- _____

Other tasks or notes

- _____

- _____

- _____

- _____

- _____

- _____

- _____

- _____

WHAT? What is going on in my life?

_____

_____

_____

_____

_____

_____

_____

SO WHAT? Why does all this matter?

_____

_____

_____

_____

> When you focus on what you lack, you lose what you have.
> When you focus on what you have, you get what you lack.
>
> —*Effortless*, p. 58

NOW WHAT? What's important now?

1 essential project

- _____

2 urgent and essential tasks

- _____

- _____

3 maintenance items

- _____

- _____

- _____

Other tasks or notes

- _____

- _____

- _____

- _____

- _____

- _____

- _____

- _____

Weekly
REFLECTION

STEP 1.
PRACTICE RADICAL GRATITUDE

Review the last week and write down five things you're
grateful for (including the tough things).

- _____

- _____

- _____

- _____

- _____

STEP 2.
PREVIEW THE WEEK

Review your calendar and write down the major events
or activities already scheduled for the coming week.

- _____

- _____

- _____

- _____

- _____

INVEST INTENTIONALLY AND DIVEST DELIBERATELY

Write down two to three essentials you're currently underinvesting in.

Write down two to three nonessentials you're currently overinvesting in.

- _____
- _____
- _____

- _____
- _____
- _____

NOW, CHOOSE THIS WEEK'S GOALS

Capture the three essential items you want to accomplish over the coming week.

- _____
- _____
- _____

WHAT? What is going on in my life?

_____

_____

_____

_____

_____

_____

SO WHAT? Why does all this matter?

_____

_____

_____

_____

> Our options may be things, but a choice . . . is an *action.* It is not just something we have but something we do. . . . While we may not always have control over our options, we *always* have control over how we choose among them.

—*Essentialism,* p. 35

NOW WHAT? What's important now?

1 essential project

- _____

2 urgent and essential tasks

- _____

- _____

3 maintenance items

- _____

- _____

- _____

Other tasks or notes

- _____

- _____

- _____

- _____

- _____

- _____

- _____

- _____

WHAT? What is going on in my life?

_____

_____

_____

_____

_____

_____

_____

SO WHAT? Why does all this matter?

_____

_____

_____

_____

TODAY'S CHALLENGE:

When your old ways of working are not working, try something new:

1. Think of something trivial you are overinvesting in.
2. Write down what it is costing you in terms of health, family, friends, important projects.
3. Decide how you will respond next time you are tempted to invest in this again.

—*1-Minute Wednesday Newsletter*

NOW WHAT? What's important now?

1 essential project

- _____

2 urgent and essential tasks

- _____

- _____

3 maintenance items

- _____

- _____

- _____

Other tasks or notes

- _____

- _____

- _____

- _____

- _____

- _____

- _____

- _____

WHAT? What is going on in my life?

_____

_____

_____

_____

_____

_____

_____

SO WHAT? Why does all this matter?

_____

_____

_____

_____

> **There are far more activities and opportunities in the world than we have time and resources to invest in. And although many of them may be good, or even very good, the fact is that most are trivial and few are vital. The way of the Essentialist involves learning to tell the difference.**
>
> —*Essentialism*, p. 5

NOW WHAT? What's important now?

1 essential project

- _____

2 urgent and essential tasks

- _____

- _____

3 maintenance items

- _____

- _____

- _____

Other tasks or notes

- _____

- _____

- _____

- _____

- _____

- _____

- _____

- _____

WHAT? What is going on in my life?

_____

_____

_____

_____

_____

_____

_____

SO WHAT? Why does all this matter?

_____

_____

_____

_____

TODAY'S CHALLENGE:

There are two opposing ways to approach an important goal or deadline. You can start early and small or start late and big. . . . "Early and small" means starting at the earliest possible moment with the minimal possible time investment. . . . Take a goal or deadline you have coming up and ask yourself, "What is the minimal amount I could do *right now* to prepare?" Spend no more than four minutes on that project today. Just start it.

—*Essentialism*, p. 200

NOW WHAT? What's important now?

1 essential project

- _____

2 urgent and essential tasks

- _____

- _____

3 maintenance items

- _____

- _____

- _____

Other tasks or notes

- _____

- _____

- _____

- _____

- _____

- _____

- _____

- _____

WHAT? What is going on in my life?

_____

_____

_____

_____

_____

_____

_____

SO WHAT? Why does all this matter?

_____

_____

_____

_____

> **Why would we simply endure essential activities when we can enjoy them instead? By pairing essential activities with enjoyable ones, we can make tackling even the most tedious and overwhelming tasks more effortless.**
>
> —*Effortless*, p. 44

NOW WHAT? What's important now?

1 essential project

- _____

2 urgent and essential tasks

- _____

- _____

3 maintenance items

- _____

- _____

- _____

Other tasks or notes

- _____

- _____

- _____

- _____

- _____

- _____

- _____

- _____

WHAT? What is going on in my life?

_____

_____

_____

_____

_____

_____

_____

SO WHAT? Why does all this matter?

_____

_____

_____

_____

TODAY'S CHALLENGE:

Say no to something today using the following strategy:

1. Evaluate the opportunity: Will I feel bad about saying no to this opportunity a year from now?
2. Focus on the trade-off: What will I be giving up if I say yes to this opportunity?
3. Remember how it feels after you say no: How did I feel last time I said no to an opportunity that wasn't right for me?

—*1-Minute Wednesday Newsletter*

NOW WHAT? What's important now?

1 essential project

- _____

2 urgent and essential tasks

- _____

- _____

3 maintenance items

- _____

- _____

- _____

Other tasks or notes

- _____

- _____

- _____

- _____

- _____

- _____

- _____

- _____

SUNDAY ___ / ___

WHAT? What is going on in my life?

_____

_____

_____

_____

_____

_____

_____

SO WHAT? Why does all this matter?

_____

_____

_____

_____

> There is no such thing as an effortless relationship. But there are ways we can make it easier to keep a relationship strong. We don't need to agree with the other person on everything. But we do need to be present with them, to really notice them, to give them our full attention—maybe not always, but as frequently as we can.
>
> —*Effortless*, p. 85

NOW WHAT? What's important now?

1 essential project

- _____

2 urgent and essential tasks

- _____

- _____

3 maintenance items

- _____

- _____

- _____

Other tasks or notes

- _____

- _____

- _____

- _____

- _____

- _____

- _____

- _____

Weekly
REFLECTION

STEP 1.
PRACTICE RADICAL GRATITUDE

Review the last week and write down five things you're
grateful for (including the tough things).

- _____

- _____

- _____

- _____

- _____

STEP 2.
PREVIEW THE WEEK

Review your calendar and write down the major events
or activities already scheduled for the coming week.

- _____

- _____

- _____

- _____

- _____

INVEST INTENTIONALLY AND DIVEST DELIBERATELY

Write down two to three essentials you're currently underinvesting in.

- _____

- _____

- _____

Write down two to three nonessentials you're currently overinvesting in.

- _____

- _____

- _____

NOW, CHOOSE THIS WEEK'S GOALS

Capture the three essential items you want to accomplish over the coming week.

- _____

- _____

- _____

WHAT? What is going on in my life?

_____

_____

_____

_____

_____

_____

_____

SO WHAT? Why does all this matter?

_____

_____

_____

_____

Essentialists see trade-offs as an inherent part of life, not as an inherently negative part of life. Instead of asking, "What do I have to give up?" they ask, "What do I want to go big on?"

—*Essentialism,* p. 56

NOW WHAT? What's important now?

1 essential project

- _____

2 urgent and essential tasks

- _____

- _____

3 maintenance items

- _____

- _____

- _____

Other tasks or notes

- _____

- _____

- _____

- _____

- _____

- _____

- _____

- _____

WHAT? What is going on in my life?

_____

_____

_____

_____

_____

_____

_____

SO WHAT? Why does all this matter?

_____

_____

_____

_____

TODAY'S CHALLENGE:

Catch someone doing something good and acknowledge them.
Compliment a partner or child. Start a work meeting by celebrating
something that is going right.

—*The Greg McKeown Podcast,* episode 260, "What's Essential: Q&A on the Power
  of Small Wins"

NOW WHAT? What's important now?

1 essential project

- _____

2 urgent and essential tasks

- _____

- _____

3 maintenance items

- _____

- _____

- _____

Other tasks or notes

- _____

- _____

- _____

- _____

- _____

- _____

- _____

- _____

WHAT? What is going on in my life?

_____

_____

_____

_____

_____

_____

_____

SO WHAT? Why does all this matter?

_____

_____

_____

_____

> Essentialism is a disciplined, systematic approach for determining where our highest point of contribution lies, then making execution of those things almost effortless.
>
> —*Essentialism*, p. 7

NOW WHAT? What's important now?

1 essential project

- _____

2 urgent and essential tasks

- _____

- _____

3 maintenance items

- _____

- _____

- _____

Other tasks or notes

- _____

- _____

- _____

- _____

- _____

- _____

- _____

- _____

WHAT? What is going on in my life?

_____

_____

_____

_____

_____

_____

_____

SO WHAT? Why does all this matter?

_____

_____

_____

_____

TODAY'S CHALLENGE:

Getting clear on what done looks like doesn't just help you finish. It helps you get started too. All too often, we procrastinate or struggle to find the first steps on a project because we don't have a clear finish line in mind. Today, identify an important project you are working on and write down what done looks like.

—*The Greg McKeown Podcast,* episode 227, "The Vasa—Define Your Done"

NOW WHAT? What's important now?

1 essential project

- _____

2 urgent and essential tasks

- _____

- _____

3 maintenance items

- _____

- _____

- _____

Other tasks or notes

- _____

- _____

- _____

- _____

- _____

- _____

- _____

- _____

WHAT? What is going on in my life?

_____

_____

_____

_____

_____

_____

_____

SO WHAT? Why does all this matter?

_____

_____

_____

_____

> Instead of asking, "Why is this so hard?," invert the question by asking, "What if this could be easy?"

—*Effortless,* p. 90

NOW WHAT? What's important now?

1 essential project

- _____

2 urgent and essential tasks

- _____

- _____

3 maintenance items

- _____

- _____

- _____

Other tasks or notes

- _____

- _____

- _____

- _____

- _____

- _____

- _____

- _____

WHAT? What is going on in my life?

SO WHAT? Why does all this matter?

TODAY'S CHALLENGE:

Think about the last week. Have you slept less than seven hours on any of those nights? The way of the Nonessentialist is to see sleep as yet another burden on one's already overextended, overcommitted, busy-but-not-always-productive life. Essentialists instead see sleep as necessary for operating at high levels of contribution more of the time. Make a plan today for scheduling more sleep into your evenings. Stick with it for the following week.

—*Essentialism*, p. 95–96

NOW WHAT? What's important now?

1 essential project

- _____

2 urgent and essential tasks

- _____

- _____

3 maintenance items

- _____

- _____

- _____

Other tasks or notes

- _____

- _____

- _____

- _____

- _____

- _____

- _____

- _____

WHAT? What is going on in my life?

_____

_____

_____

_____

_____

_____

_____

SO WHAT? Why does all this matter?

_____

_____

_____

_____

> We aren't looking for a plethora of good things to do. We are looking for our highest level of contribution: the right thing the right way at the right time.
>
> —_Essentialism_, p. 22

NOW WHAT? What's important now?

1 essential project

- _____

2 urgent and essential tasks

- _____

- _____

3 maintenance items

- _____

- _____

- _____

Other tasks or notes

- _____

- _____

- _____

- _____

- _____

- _____

- _____

- _____

Weekly

REFLECTION

STEP 1.
PRACTICE RADICAL GRATITUDE

Review the last week and write down five things you're
grateful for (including the tough things).

- _____

- _____

- _____

- _____

- _____

STEP 2.
PREVIEW THE WEEK

Review your calendar and write down the major events
or activities already scheduled for the coming week.

- _____

- _____

- _____

- _____

- _____

INVEST INTENTIONALLY AND DIVEST DELIBERATELY

Write down two to three essentials you're currently underinvesting in.

- _____

- _____

- _____

Write down two to three nonessentials you're currently overinvesting in.

- _____

- _____

- _____

NOW, CHOOSE THIS WEEK'S GOALS

Capture the three essential items you want to accomplish over the coming week.

- _____

- _____

- _____

WHAT? What is going on in my life?

_____

_____

_____

_____

_____

_____

SO WHAT? Why does all this matter?

_____

_____

_____

_____

> Have you ever continued to invest time or effort in a nonessential project instead of cutting your losses? Have you ever continued to pour money into an investment that wasn't panning out instead of walking away? . . . A Nonessentialist can't break free of traps like these. An Essentialist has the courage and confidence to admit his or her mistakes and uncommit, no matter the sunk costs.
>
> —*Essentialism*, p. 147

NOW WHAT? What's important now?

1 essential project

- _____

2 urgent and essential tasks

- _____

- _____

3 maintenance items

- _____

- _____

- _____

Other tasks or notes

- _____

- _____

- _____

- _____

- _____

- _____

- _____

- _____

- _____

WHAT? What is going on in my life?

_____

_____

_____

_____

_____

_____

_____

SO WHAT? Why does all this matter?

_____

_____

_____

_____

TODAY'S CHALLENGE:

Progress can happen in tiny increments. Two and a half seconds is enough time to shift your focus, put your phone down, close the browser, or take a deep breath. . . . Try this:

1. Make a list of "go-to" micro-actions you can turn to when you notice yourself being unproductive (e.g., put your phone down, get out your planner, stand up and walk outside).
2. Keep this list somewhere you will see it often.
3. Use it when you begin to feel unproductive or distracted.

—1-Minute Wednesday Newsletter

NOW WHAT? What's important now?

1 essential project

- _____

2 urgent and essential tasks

- _____

- _____

3 maintenance items

- _____

- _____

- _____

Other tasks or notes

- _____

- _____

- _____

- _____

- _____

- _____

- _____

- _____

WHAT? What is going on in my life?

_____

_____

_____

_____

_____

_____

_____

SO WHAT? Why does all this matter?

_____

_____

_____

_____

As you evaluate an option, think about the single most important criterion for that decision, and then simply give the option a score between 0 and 100. If you rate it any lower than 90 percent, then automatically change the rating to 0 and simply reject it. This way you avoid getting caught up in indecision, or worse, getting stuck with the 60s or 70s.

—*Essentialism,* p. 105

NOW WHAT? What's important now?

1 essential project

- _____

2 urgent and essential tasks

- _____

- _____

3 maintenance items

- _____

- _____

- _____

Other tasks or notes

- _____

- _____

- _____

- _____

- _____

- _____

- _____

- _____

WHAT? What is going on in my life?

_____

_____

_____

_____

_____

_____

_____

SO WHAT? Why does all this matter?

_____

_____

_____

_____

TODAY'S CHALLENGE:

Do not do more today than you can completely recover from today. Do the following: 1) dedicate mornings to essential work; 2) break down that work into three sessions of no more than 90 minutes each; 3) take a short ten- to fifteen-minute break in between sessions to rest and recover.

—*The Greg McKeown Podcast,* episode 51, "What's Essential: Greg on the Art of Doing Nothing"

NOW WHAT? What's important now?

1 essential project

- _____

2 urgent and essential tasks

- _____

- _____

3 maintenance items

- _____

- _____

- _____

Other tasks or notes

- _____

- _____

- _____

- _____

- _____

- _____

- _____

- _____

WHAT? What is going on in my life?

_____

_____

_____

_____

_____

_____

SO WHAT? Why does all this matter?

_____

_____

_____

_____

> When people ask us to do something, we can confuse the request with our relationship with them. . . . Only once we separate the decision from the relationship can we make a clear decision and then separately find the courage and compassion to communicate it.
>
> —*Essentialism*, p. 137

NOW WHAT? What's important now?

1 essential project

- _____

2 urgent and essential tasks

- _____

- _____

3 maintenance items

- _____

- _____

- _____

Other tasks or notes

- _____

- _____

- _____

- _____

- _____

- _____

- _____

- _____

WHAT? What is going on in my life?

_____

_____

_____

_____

_____

_____

_____

SO WHAT? Why does all this matter?

_____

_____

_____

_____

TODAY'S CHALLENGE:

I have a friend who takes a fantastic approach to failure. As a Spanish teacher, he teaches his students to imagine having a bag of 1,000 beads. Every time they make a mistake when speaking Spanish, they remove a bead from the bag. When the bag is empty, they have achieved a level 1 mastery. Try your own version of this exercise. Think of something you want to master and see making mistakes early as a way to accelerate learning.

—_1-Minute Wednesday Newsletter_

NOW WHAT? What's important now?

1 essential project

- _____

2 urgent and essential tasks

- _____

- _____

3 maintenance items

- _____

- _____

- _____

Other tasks or notes

- _____

- _____

- _____

- _____

- _____

- _____

- _____

- _____

WHAT? What is going on in my life?

_____

_____

_____

_____

_____

_____

_____

SO WHAT? Why does all this matter?

_____

_____

_____

_____

> Essentialists *choose* "no" more often than they *say* no. . . . Whether it's "I am flattered that you thought of me but I'm afraid I don't have the bandwidth" or "I would very much like to but I'm overcommitted," there are a variety of ways of refusing someone clearly and politely without actually using the word *no*.
>
> —*Essentialism*, p. 137

NOW WHAT? What's important now?

1 essential project

- _____

2 urgent and essential tasks

- _____

- _____

3 maintenance items

- _____

- _____

- _____

Other tasks or notes

- _____

- _____

- _____

- _____

- _____

- _____

- _____

- _____

Weekly
REFLECTION

STEP 1.
PRACTICE RADICAL GRATITUDE

Review the last week and write down five things you're
grateful for (including the tough things).

- _____

- _____

- _____

- _____

- _____

STEP 2.
PREVIEW THE WEEK

Review your calendar and write down the major events
or activities already scheduled for the coming week.

- _____

- _____

- _____

- _____

- _____

INVEST INTENTIONALLY AND DIVEST DELIBERATELY

Write down two to three essentials you're currently underinvesting in.

Write down two to three nonessentials you're currently overinvesting in.

- _____
- _____
- _____

- _____
- _____
- _____

NOW, CHOOSE THIS WEEK'S GOALS

Capture the three essential items you want to accomplish over the coming week.

- _____
- _____
- _____

WHAT? What is going on in my life?

_____

_____

_____

_____

_____

_____

_____

SO WHAT? Why does all this matter?

_____

_____

_____

_____

> *The pursuit of success can be a catalyst for failure.* Put another way, success can distract us from focusing on the essential things that produce success in the first place.

—*Essentialism*, p. 13

NOW WHAT? What's important now?

1 essential project

- _____

2 urgent and essential tasks

- _____
- _____

3 maintenance items

- _____
- _____
- _____

Other tasks or notes

- _____
- _____
- _____
- _____
- _____
- _____
- _____
- _____

TUESDAY __ / __

WHAT? What is going on in my life?

_____

_____

_____

_____

_____

_____

_____

SO WHAT? Why does all this matter?

_____

_____

_____

_____

TODAY'S CHALLENGE:

Sometimes we find it hard to say no because we forget that every yes comes with a trade-off. This week focus on the trade-offs you are making. Every time you say yes to one opportunity, cross off something on your calendar that you will now need to say no to.

—1-Minute Wednesday Newsletter

138

NOW WHAT? What's important now?

1 essential project

- _____

2 urgent and essential tasks

- _____

- _____

3 maintenance items

- _____

- _____

- _____

Other tasks or notes

- _____

- _____

- _____

- _____

- _____

- _____

- _____

- _____

WHAT? What is going on in my life?

_____

_____

_____

_____

_____

_____

_____

SO WHAT? Why does all this matter?

_____

_____

_____

_____

> **What if the biggest thing keeping us from doing what matters is the false assumption that it has to take tremendous effort? What if, instead, we considered the possibility that the reason something feels hard is that we haven't yet found the easier way to do it?**
>
> —*Effortless*, p. 29

NOW WHAT? What's important now?

1 essential project

- _____

2 urgent and essential tasks

- _____

- _____

3 maintenance items

- _____

- _____

- _____

Other tasks or notes

- _____

- _____

- _____

- _____

- _____

- _____

- _____

- _____

WHAT? What is going on in my life?

_____

_____

_____

_____

_____

_____

_____

SO WHAT? Why does all this matter?

_____

_____

_____

_____

TODAY'S CHALLENGE:

Our growth, our fulfillment, and our very potential are interwoven with our connection to others. Connect with someone today. A few ideas:

- Perform an act of kindness for a stranger.
- Help someone you lead or mentor solve a problem.
- Reconnect with a friend or family member.
- Contribute to a community project.

—1-Minute Wednesday Newsletter

NOW WHAT? What's important now?

1 essential project

- _____

2 urgent and essential tasks

- _____

- _____

3 maintenance items

- _____

- _____

- _____

Other tasks or notes

- _____

- _____

- _____

- _____

- _____

- _____

- _____

- _____

WHAT? What is going on in my life?

_____

_____

_____

_____

_____

_____

_____

SO WHAT? Why does all this matter?

_____

_____

_____

_____

> **When a strategy is so complex that each step feels akin to pushing a boulder up a hill, you should pause. Invert the problem. Ask, "What's the simplest way to achieve this result?"**
>
> —*Effortless*, p. 39

NOW WHAT? What's important now?

1 essential project

- _____

2 urgent and essential tasks

- _____

- _____

3 maintenance items

- _____

- _____

- _____

Other tasks or notes

- _____

- _____

- _____

- _____

- _____

- _____

- _____

- _____

WHAT? What is going on in my life?

_____

_____

_____

_____

_____

_____

_____

SO WHAT? Why does all this matter?

_____

_____

_____

_____

TODAY'S CHALLENGE:

Select a book of classic literature to read. As you read, think about what you are learning and how you can leverage those ideas in your life. Ask yourself, "What do I read most? News sites? Social media? Brain candy fiction? How would my thinking change if I replaced that reading with the classics?"

—*The Greg McKeown Podcast,* episode 243, "The Best of What Others Know"

NOW WHAT? What's important now?

1 essential project

- _____

2 urgent and essential tasks

- _____

- _____

3 maintenance items

- _____

- _____

- _____

Other tasks or notes

- _____

- _____

- _____

- _____

- _____

- _____

- _____

- _____

WHAT? What is going on in my life?

_____

_____

_____

_____

_____

_____

_____

SO WHAT? Why does all this matter?

_____

_____

_____

_____

> **Essentialists spend as much time as possible exploring, listening, debating, questioning, and thinking. But their exploration is not an end in itself. The purpose of the exploration is to discern the vital few from the trivial many.**
>
> —_Essentialism_, p. 22

NOW WHAT? What's important now?

1 essential project

- _____

2 urgent and essential tasks

- _____

- _____

3 maintenance items

- _____

- _____

- _____

Other tasks or notes

- _____

- _____

- _____

- _____

- _____

- _____

- _____

- _____

Weekly
REFLECTION

STEP 1.
PRACTICE RADICAL GRATITUDE

Review the last week and write down five things you're
grateful for (including the tough things).

- _____

- _____

- _____

- _____

- _____

STEP 2.
PREVIEW THE WEEK

Review your calendar and write down the major events
or activities already scheduled for the coming week.

- _____

- _____

- _____

- _____

- _____

STEP 3.
INVEST INTENTIONALLY AND DIVEST DELIBERATELY

Write down two to three essentials you're currently underinvesting in.

- _____
- _____
- _____

Write down two to three nonessentials you're currently overinvesting in.

- _____
- _____
- _____

STEP 4.
NOW, CHOOSE THIS WEEK'S GOALS

Capture the three essential items you want to accomplish over the coming week.

- _____
- _____
- _____

WHAT? What is going on in my life?

_____

_____

_____

_____

_____

_____

SO WHAT? Why does all this matter?

_____

_____

_____

_____

Working hard is important. But more effort does not necessarily yield more results. "Less but better" does.

—*Essentialism*, p. 43

NOW WHAT? What's important now?

1 essential project

- _____

2 urgent and essential tasks

- _____

- _____

3 maintenance items

- _____

- _____

- _____

Other tasks or notes

- _____

- _____

- _____

- _____

- _____

- _____

- _____

- _____

- _____

TUESDAY ___ / ___

WHAT? What is going on in my life?

_____

_____

_____

_____

_____

_____

_____

SO WHAT? Why does all this matter?

_____

_____

_____

_____

TODAY'S CHALLENGE:

Many of us are nervous to tell our boss or an important client no. But you don't have to. Instead, today practice asking a second-order question to create dialogue around what to prioritize, such as: "Here is what I'm working on. What would you like me to deprioritize?"

—*1-Minute Wednesday Newsletter*

NOW WHAT? What's important now?

1 essential project

- _____

2 urgent and essential tasks

- _____

- _____

3 maintenance items

- _____

- _____

- _____

Other tasks or notes

- _____

- _____

- _____

- _____

- _____

- _____

- _____

- _____

WHAT? What is going on in my life?

_____

_____

_____

_____

_____

_____

_____

SO WHAT? Why does all this matter?

_____

_____

_____

_____

To see others more clearly, set aside your opinions, advice, and judgment, and put their truth above your own.

—*Effortless*, p. 91

NOW WHAT? What's important now?

1 essential project

- _____

2 urgent and essential tasks

- _____

- _____

3 maintenance items

- _____

- _____

- _____

Other tasks or notes

- _____

- _____

- _____

- _____

- _____

- _____

- _____

- _____

WHAT? What is going on in my life?

_____

_____

_____

_____

_____

_____

_____

SO WHAT? Why does all this matter?

_____

_____

_____

_____

TODAY'S CHALLENGE:

When you come up against a challenge today, ask yourself, "How am I making things harder than they need to be?" When you have your answer to that question you will have something of great value: you will know what to do next. It is as simple, and it might just be as easy, as that.

—*1-Minute Wednesday Newsletter*

NOW WHAT? What's important now?

1 essential project

- _____

2 urgent and essential tasks

- _____

- _____

3 maintenance items

- _____

- _____

- _____

Other tasks or notes

- _____

- _____

- _____

- _____

- _____

- _____

- _____

- _____

WHAT? What is going on in my life?

_____

_____

_____

_____

_____

_____

_____

SO WHAT? Why does all this matter?

_____

_____

_____

_____

People tend to think of focus as a thing. Yes, focus is something we have. But focus is also something we _do_. In order to _have_ focus we need to escape _to_ focus.

—*Essentialism,* p. 66

NOW WHAT? What's important now?

1 essential project

- _____

2 urgent and essential tasks

- _____

- _____

3 maintenance items

- _____

- _____

- _____

Other tasks or notes

- _____

- _____

- _____

- _____

- _____

- _____

- _____

- _____

SATURDAY ___ / ___

WHAT? What is going on in my life?

_____

_____

_____

_____

_____

_____

_____

SO WHAT? Why does all this matter?

_____

_____

_____

_____

TODAY'S CHALLENGE:

Curiosity is more than just a personality trait. True curiosity, the kind that breeds innovation and discovery, is an intentional choice in the way we live. To do this, ask more questions: Whether you are in a conversation with colleagues, a job interview, or speaking with a friend or partner, go deeper into the conversation by asking the second and third questions.

—_The Greg McKeown Podcast,_ episode 219, "Curiosity Is a Discipline"

NOW WHAT? What's important now?

1 essential project

- _____

2 urgent and essential tasks

- _____

- _____

3 maintenance items

- _____

- _____

- _____

Other tasks or notes

- _____

- _____

- _____

- _____

- _____

- _____

- _____

- _____

WHAT? What is going on in my life?

_____

_____

_____

_____

_____

_____

_____

SO WHAT? Why does all this matter?

_____

_____

_____

_____

> Have you ever found that the more you complain—and the more you read and hear other people complain—the easier it is to find things to complain about? On the other hand, have you ever found that the more grateful you are, the more you have to be grateful for?
>
> —*Effortless*, p. 55

NOW WHAT? What's important now?

1 essential project

- _____

2 urgent and essential tasks

- _____

- _____

3 maintenance items

- _____

- _____

- _____

Other tasks or notes

- _____

- _____

- _____

- _____

- _____

- _____

- _____

- _____

Weekly
REFLECTION

STEP 1.
PRACTICE RADICAL GRATITUDE

Review the last week and write down five things you're
grateful for (including the tough things).

- _____
- _____
- _____
- _____
- _____

STEP 2.
PREVIEW THE WEEK

Review your calendar and write down the major events
or activities already scheduled for the coming week.

- _____
- _____
- _____
- _____
- _____

INVEST INTENTIONALLY AND DIVEST DELIBERATELY

Write down two to three essentials you're currently underinvesting in.

- _____

- _____

- _____

Write down two to three nonessentials you're currently overinvesting in.

- _____

- _____

- _____

NOW, CHOOSE THIS WEEK'S GOALS

Capture the three essential items you want to accomplish over the coming week.

- _____

- _____

- _____

WHAT? What is going on in my life?

_____

_____

_____

_____

_____

_____

SO WHAT? Why does all this matter?

_____

_____

_____

_____

Our highest priority is to protect our ability to prioritize.

—*Essentialism,* p. 101

NOW WHAT? What's important now?

1 essential project

- _____

2 urgent and essential tasks

- _____

- _____

3 maintenance items

- _____

- _____

- _____

Other tasks or notes

- _____

- _____

- _____

- _____

- _____

- _____

- _____

- _____

WHAT? What is going on in my life?

_____

_____

_____

_____

_____

_____

_____

SO WHAT? Why does all this matter?

_____

_____

_____

_____

TODAY'S CHALLENGE:

Routine is one of the most powerful tools for removing obstacles. Without routine, the pull of nonessential distractions will overpower us. But if we create a routine that enshrines the essentials, we will begin to execute them on autopilot. How can you leverage your daily routine to eliminate everyday obstacles and avoid decision fatigue—whether it's automating what you wear or what you eat—so you can devote more of your mental activity to something more essential?

—*Essentialism,* p. 206

NOW WHAT? What's important now?

1 essential project

- _____

2 urgent and essential tasks

- _____

- _____

3 maintenance items

- _____

- _____

- _____

Other tasks or notes

- _____

- _____

- _____

- _____

- _____

- _____

- _____

- _____

WHAT? What is going on in my life?

_____

_____

_____

_____

_____

_____

_____

SO WHAT? Why does all this matter?

_____

_____

_____

_____

Past a certain point, more effort doesn't produce better performance. It sabotages our performance. Economists call this the law of diminishing returns.

—*Effortless,* p. 95

NOW WHAT? What's important now?

1 essential project

- _____

2 urgent and essential tasks

- _____

- _____

3 maintenance items

- _____

- _____

- _____

Other tasks or notes

- _____

- _____

- _____

- _____

- _____

- _____

- _____

- _____

WHAT? What is going on in my life?

_____

_____

_____

_____

_____

_____

_____

SO WHAT? Why does all this matter?

_____

_____

_____

_____

TODAY'S CHALLENGE:

The key to our success lies in learning from our past. To help you remember and reflect on your experience, keep a daily journal (you can use the space above to journal). But instead of focusing on every detail of your day, focus on two or three important things, such as:

- What was something that happened that you want to remember?
- What was something you learned?
- What was something you were grateful for?

—1-Minute Wednesday Newsletter

NOW WHAT? What's important now?

1 essential project

- _____

2 urgent and essential tasks

- _____

- _____

3 maintenance items

- _____

- _____

- _____

Other tasks or notes

- _____

- _____

- _____

- _____

- _____

- _____

- _____

- _____

WHAT? What is going on in my life?

_____

_____

_____

_____

_____

_____

SO WHAT? Why does all this matter?

_____

_____

_____

_____

Evading hard questions can be tempting for us all. Often it's easier to give a vague, blanket answer rather than to summon up the facts and information required to give a thoughtful, informed answer. Yet evasiveness only sends us down a nonessential spiral of further vagueness and misinformation. Clarifying the question is a way out of that cycle.

—*Essentialism,* p. 80

NOW WHAT? What's important now?

1 essential project

- _____

2 urgent and essential tasks

- _____

- _____

3 maintenance items

- _____

- _____

- _____

Other tasks or notes

- _____

- _____

- _____

- _____

- _____

- _____

- _____

- _____

WHAT? What is going on in my life?

_____

_____

_____

_____

_____

_____

_____

SO WHAT? Why does all this matter?

_____

_____

_____

_____

TODAY'S CHALLENGE:

A lack of consistent, recognizable landmarks often hampers your ability to make meaningful progress. You must do all you can to remove the trivial things in your life that are blocking your view of the essential few. To ensure you continue to make progress, try this:

1. Identify one "landmark" and answer these questions:
   - What do I need to do today to move toward this goal? This week? This month? This quarter?
   - What trivial things are obscuring my view?

2. Once per quarter, take time to evaluate your progress—and course-correct if necessary.

—1-Minute Wednesday Newsletter

NOW WHAT? What's important now?

1 essential project

- _____

2 urgent and essential tasks

- _____

- _____

3 maintenance items

- _____

- _____

- _____

Other tasks or notes

- _____

- _____

- _____

- _____

- _____

- _____

- _____

- _____

WHAT? What is going on in my life?

_____

_____

_____

_____

_____

_____

_____

SO WHAT? Why does all this matter?

_____

_____

_____

_____

If [you] could be truly excellent at only one thing, what would it be?

—*Essentialism,* p. 127

NOW WHAT? What's important now?

1 essential project

- _____

2 urgent and essential tasks

- _____

- _____

3 maintenance items

- _____

- _____

- _____

Other tasks or notes

- _____

- _____

- _____

- _____

- _____

- _____

- _____

- _____

REFLECTION

STEP 1.
PRACTICE RADICAL GRATITUDE

Review the last week and write down five things you're
grateful for (including the tough things).

- _____

- _____

- _____

- _____

- _____

STEP 2.
PREVIEW THE WEEK

Review your calendar and write down the major events
or activities already scheduled for the coming week.

- _____

- _____

- _____

- _____

- _____

INVEST INTENTIONALLY AND DIVEST DELIBERATELY

Write down two to three essentials you're currently underinvesting in.

Write down two to three nonessentials you're currently overinvesting in.

- _____
- _____
- _____

- _____
- _____
- _____

NOW, CHOOSE THIS WEEK'S GOALS

Capture the three essential items you want to accomplish over the coming week.

- _____
- _____
- _____

WHAT? What is going on in my life?

_____

_____

_____

_____

_____

_____

_____

SO WHAT? Why does all this matter?

_____

_____

_____

_____

> Strangely, some of us respond to feeling exhausted and overwhelmed by vowing to work even harder and longer. It doesn't help that our culture glorifies burnout as a measure of success and self-worth. . . . Burnout is not a badge of honor.
>
> —*Effortless*, p. 7

NOW WHAT? What's important now?

1 essential project

- _____

2 urgent and essential tasks

- _____

- _____

3 maintenance items

- _____

- _____

- _____

Other tasks or notes

- _____

- _____

- _____

- _____

- _____

- _____

- _____

- _____

WHAT? What is going on in my life?

_____

_____

_____

_____

_____

_____

SO WHAT? Why does all this matter?

_____

_____

_____

_____

TODAY'S CHALLENGE:

Loss aversion is the idea that we perceive the pain of losing something as more significant than the joy of gaining something else. To help you uncommit, use this strategy suggested by the BBC's Tom Stafford:

- Think of something (an object or responsibility) that you're afraid of losing.
- Pretend you don't own it and ask yourself, "How much would I pay to obtain this?"
- When it comes to nonmaterial things ask, "How hard would I work to get involved if I wasn't already involved?"

—_1-Minute Wednesday Newsletter_

NOW WHAT? What's important now?

1 essential project

- _____

2 urgent and essential tasks

- _____

- _____

3 maintenance items

- _____

- _____

- _____

Other tasks or notes

- _____

- _____

- _____

- _____

- _____

- _____

- _____

- _____

WHAT? What is going on in my life?

_____

_____

_____

_____

_____

_____

_____

SO WHAT? Why does all this matter?

_____

_____

_____

_____

> We all have some people in our lives who tend to be higher maintenance for us than others. These are the people who make their problem our problem. They distract us from our purpose. . . . But when people make their problem our problem, we aren't helping them; we're enabling them. Once we take their problem for them, all we're doing is taking away their ability to solve it.

—*Essentialism*, p. 167–68

NOW WHAT? What's important now?

1 essential project

- _____

2 urgent and essential tasks

- _____

- _____

3 maintenance items

- _____

- _____

- _____

Other tasks or notes

- _____

- _____

- _____

- _____

- _____

- _____

- _____

- _____

WHAT? What is going on in my life?

_____

_____

_____

_____

_____

_____

_____

SO WHAT? Why does all this matter?

_____

_____

_____

_____

TODAY'S CHALLENGE:

The highest-performing teams have one thing in common—psychological safety. This week, use this three-step process to introduce greater psychological safety into difficult conversations:

1. State what your intent is not.
2. State what your intent is.
3. Ask the magic question, "Are we willing to chat until, together, we find a solution that's better than what either party has been suggesting or doing in the past?"

—*The Greg McKeown Podcast,* episode 140, "One Phrase for Achieving Psychological Safety"

NOW WHAT? What's important now?

1 essential project

- _____

2 urgent and essential tasks

- _____

- _____

3 maintenance items

- _____

- _____

- _____

Other tasks or notes

- _____

- _____

- _____

- _____

- _____

- _____

- _____

- _____

WHAT? What is going on in my life?

_____

_____

_____

_____

_____

_____

SO WHAT? Why does all this matter?

_____

_____

_____

_____

There are two ways of thinking about Essentialism. The first is to think of it as something you *do* occasionally. The second is to think of it as something you *are*. In the former, Essentialism is one more thing to add to your already overstuffed life. In the latter, it is a different way—a simpler way—of doing everything.

—*Essentialism,* p. 226

NOW WHAT? What's important now?

1 essential project

- _____

2 urgent and essential tasks

- _____

- _____

3 maintenance items

- _____

- _____

- _____

Other tasks or notes

- _____

- _____

- _____

- _____

- _____

- _____

- _____

- _____

WHAT? What is going on in my life?

_____

_____

_____

_____

_____

_____

_____

SO WHAT? Why does all this matter?

_____

_____

_____

_____

TODAY'S CHALLENGE:

Regret can play an inspiring role to help us make better choices in the future. Follow this process to let a regret fuel a positive change in your life:

- Name a regret you have.
- Look at the gap between what you wish it had been and what it has actually been.
- Envision what the future will be if you don't make a change.
- Use the space you have to do something different.

—*The Greg McKeown Podcast*, episode 160, "It's Not Too Late"

NOW WHAT? What's important now?

1 essential project

- _____

2 urgent and essential tasks

- _____

- _____

3 maintenance items

- _____

- _____

- _____

Other tasks or notes

- _____

- _____

- _____

- _____

- _____

- _____

- _____

- _____

WHAT? What is going on in my life?

_____

_____

_____

_____

_____

_____

_____

SO WHAT? Why does all this matter?

_____

_____

_____

_____

> The way of the Essentialist isn't just about success; it's about living a life of meaning and purpose. When we look back on our careers and our lives, would we rather see a long laundry list of "accomplishments" that don't really matter or just a few major accomplishments that have real meaning and significance?
>
> —*Essentialism*, p. 230

NOW WHAT? What's important now?

1 essential project

- _____

2 urgent and essential tasks

- _____

- _____

3 maintenance items

- _____

- _____

- _____

Other tasks or notes

- _____

- _____

- _____

- _____

- _____

- _____

- _____

- _____

Weekly
REFLECTION

STEP 1.
PRACTICE RADICAL GRATITUDE

Review the last week and write down five things you're
grateful for (including the tough things).

- _____
- _____
- _____
- _____
- _____

STEP 2.
PREVIEW THE WEEK

Review your calendar and write down the major events
or activities already scheduled for the coming week.

- _____
- _____
- _____
- _____
- _____

INVEST INTENTIONALLY AND DIVEST DELIBERATELY

Write down two to three essentials you're currently underinvesting in.

Write down two to three nonessentials you're currently overinvesting in.

- _____
- _____
- _____

- _____
- _____
- _____

NOW, CHOOSE THIS WEEK'S GOALS

Capture the three essential items you want to accomplish over the coming week.

- _____
- _____
- _____

WHAT? What is going on in my life?

_____

_____

_____

_____

_____

_____

SO WHAT? Why does all this matter?

_____

_____

_____

_____

> **With the focus on what is truly important *right now* comes the ability to live life more fully, in the moment.**
>
> —*Essentialism,* p. 235

NOW WHAT? What's important now?

1 essential project

- _____

2 urgent and essential tasks

- _____

- _____

3 maintenance items

- _____

- _____

- _____

Other tasks or notes

- _____

- _____

- _____

- _____

- _____

- _____

- _____

- _____

WHAT? What is going on in my life?

_____

_____

_____

_____

_____

_____

_____

SO WHAT? Why does all this matter?

_____

_____

_____

_____

TODAY'S CHALLENGE:

In a world of unpredictability, we should expect the unexpected to be a guaranteed guest. We can prepare for the unexpected by building in a buffer to our essential tasks and projects. This week, build in 50% buffer time to your most important tasks. Consider a 100% to 200% buffer time for major life transitions.

—*The Greg McKeown Podcast,* episode 211, "Essentialism and Transitions"

NOW WHAT? What's important now?

1 essential project

- _____

2 urgent and essential tasks

- _____

- _____

3 maintenance items

- _____

- _____

- _____

Other tasks or notes

- _____

- _____

- _____

- _____

- _____

- _____

- _____

- _____

WHAT? What is going on in my life?

_____

_____

_____

_____

_____

_____

_____

SO WHAT? Why does all this matter?

_____

_____

_____

_____

> Essentialists are powerful observers and listeners. Knowing that the reality of trade-offs means they can't possibly pay attention to everything, they listen deliberately for what is not being explicitly stated. They read between the lines. . . . Nonessentialists listen too. But they listen while preparing to say something. They get distracted by extraneous noise. . . . In their eagerness to react they miss the point.
>
> —*Essentialism,* p. 77

NOW WHAT? What's important now?

1 essential project

- _____

2 urgent and essential tasks

- _____

- _____

3 maintenance items

- _____

- _____

- _____

Other tasks or notes

- _____

- _____

- _____

- _____

- _____

- _____

- _____

- _____

WHAT? What is going on in my life?

SO WHAT? Why does all this matter?

TODAY'S CHALLENGE:

You get to choose whether FOMO (the fear of missing out) hurts or serves you by following these tiny steps:

1. Notice the next time you are feeling FOMO.
2. Ask, "Is this just jealousy or could it be revealing something I am feeling called to do?"
3. Take one minute to schedule white space on your calendar this week to explore this in more depth.

—1-Minute Wednesday Newsletter

NOW WHAT? What's important now?

1 essential project

- _____

2 urgent and essential tasks

- _____

- _____

3 maintenance items

- _____

- _____

- _____

Other tasks or notes

- _____

- _____

- _____

- _____

- _____

- _____

- _____

- _____

WHAT? What is going on in my life?

_____
_____
_____
_____
_____
_____
_____

SO WHAT? Why does all this matter?

_____
_____
_____
_____

When faced with so many tasks and obligations that you can't figure out which to tackle first, stop. Take a deep breath. Get present in the moment and ask yourself what is most important this very second—not what's most important tomorrow or even an hour from now. If you're not sure, make a list of everything vying for your attention and cross off anything that is not important *right now.*

—*Essentialism*, p. 221

NOW WHAT? What's important now?

1 essential project

- _____

2 urgent and essential tasks

- _____

- _____

3 maintenance items

- _____

- _____

- _____

Other tasks or notes

- _____

- _____

- _____

- _____

- _____

- _____

- _____

- _____

WHAT? What is going on in my life?

_____

_____

_____

_____

_____

_____

_____

SO WHAT? Why does all this matter?

_____

_____

_____

_____

TODAY'S CHALLENGE:

Have you ever had a day where you were focused but then got one bad email that just popped your bubble of productivity? The **1-Minute Reset** can get you back on track. Here's how:

1. Create a page full of positive truths about your life (i.e., key accomplishments in your life, evidence of growth, or favorite memories).
2. When you start feeling emotionally flooded, pull out your page and read it through for one minute.

—_1-Minute Wednesday Newsletter_

NOW WHAT? What's important now?

1 essential project

- _____

2 urgent and essential tasks

- _____

- _____

3 maintenance items

- _____

- _____

- _____

Other tasks or notes

- _____

- _____

- _____

- _____

- _____

- _____

- _____

- _____

WHAT? What is going on in my life?

_____

_____

_____

_____

_____

_____

_____

SO WHAT? Why does all this matter?

_____

_____

_____

_____

> Play expands our minds in ways that allow us to explore: to germinate new ideas or see old ideas in a new light. It makes us more inquisitive, more attuned to novelty, more engaged.
>
> —*Essentialism*, p. 86

NOW WHAT? What's important now?

1 essential project

- _____

2 urgent and essential tasks

- _____

- _____

3 maintenance items

- _____

- _____

- _____

Other tasks or notes

- _____

- _____

- _____

- _____

- _____

- _____

- _____

- _____

REFLECTION

PRACTICE RADICAL GRATITUDE

Review the last week and write down five things you're
grateful for (including the tough things).

- _____
- _____
- _____
- _____
- _____

STEP 2.
PREVIEW THE WEEK

Review your calendar and write down the major events
or activities already scheduled for the coming week.

- _____
- _____
- _____
- _____
- _____

INVEST INTENTIONALLY AND DIVEST DELIBERATELY

Write down two to three essentials you're currently underinvesting in.

- _____

- _____

- _____

Write down two to three nonessentials you're currently overinvesting in.

- _____

- _____

- _____

NOW, CHOOSE THIS WEEK'S GOALS

Capture the three essential items you want to accomplish over the coming week.

- _____

- _____

- _____

RESOURCES

For more inspiration and information on Essentialism and for further reading, check out the following sources:

Essentialism and *Effortless*

Read my *New York Times* bestselling books that together have sold two million copies and have been translated into 37 languages. Visit my website to sign up and receive a free chapter from each book.

gregmckeown.com

1-Minute Wednesday Newsletter

Sign up for my weekly newsletter and read back issues at:

gregmckeown.com/1mw

The Greg McKeown Podcast

Listen to my weekly podcast for inspired weekly conversations focused on learning how to put what matters to you first and how to do less, but better.

gregmckeown.com/podcast

The Essentialism Academy

This series of powerful courses and tools is designed to help you dive deeper into my philosophy with video instruction, clear daily steps, and printable resources. Sign up at:

Essentialism.com

Also available from *New York Times* bestselling author

Greg McKeown

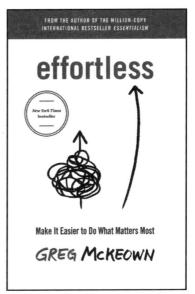

"In a world beset by burnout,
Greg McKeown's work is essential."

—DANIEL H. PINK, author of *Drive*

NOTES

Published in the United States by Clarkson Potter/Publishers, an imprint
of Random House, a division of Penguin Random House LLC, New York.

clarksonpotter.com

CLARKSON POTTER is a trademark and POTTER with colophon is a registered
trademark of Penguin Random House LLC.

This work is based on and directly quotes from *Essentialism* by Greg McKeown,
copyright © 2014, 2020 by Greg McKeown. Published in hardcover in the United
States by Crown Business and in trade paperback by Currency, both imprints of
the Crown Publishing Group, a division of Penguin Random House LLC, New
York, in 2014 and 2020 respectively. In addition, this work contains material that
originally appeared in the author's newsletters and podcast.

Library of Congress Cataloging-in-Publication Data is available upon request.

ISBN 978-0-593-57841-4

Printed in Malaysia

Editor: Angelin Adams
Editorial Assistant: Darian Keels
Designers: Maria Elias and Danielle Deschenes
Production Editor: Serena Wang
Production Manager: Luisa Francavilla

10 9 8 7 6 5 4 3 2 1

First Edition